FIFTY MISSIONS over EUROPE

Alan Shular

DIAMOND MEDIA PRESS CO.
1-747-998-2352
https://www.diamondmediapressco.com/

ISBN Paperback: 978-1951-302-42-9

CONTENTS

DEDICATION

This book is dedicated to the memory of Major John Shu-lar. He was a war hero, a son, a brother, a husband, a father, a coach, and a grandfather. He lived for his country, his family, and his students. This book is a huge indication as to what kind of a man he truly was. He rarely did anything for himself, and so for that, this book allows his memory to live on forever. We love and miss you every day dad. Love Alan, Aunt Rose, and Jesse.

FOREWORD

John Shular was born on November 30, 1915, the second of four children. John's mother and father, John and Mary Shular, both immigrated to the United States from their native Slovenia in the early years of the twentieth century. John's father found work in the coal mining camps of southeastern Kansas. When coal was still plentiful in that part of the state, one of the larger mining camps in the area was Gross, now a part of rural Arcadia, Kansas. It was there that John and his siblings (Mary, Felix, and Rose) grew up. John's mother and father were determined to see that their four children would receive the education that had not been available to them in Slovenia. Hard study was stressed in their home as much as hard work. Because of this, all four Shular children graduated from the Kansas State Teacher's College (now Pittsburg State University) in Pittsburg, Kansas. John received a Bachelor of Science degree in biology from there in 1941.

John, his brother, and his sisters all entered the teaching profession upon graduation, and John was teaching school at the time the United States entered the Second World War.

It was during his college years that John nurtured his interest in flying, hitchhiking to the local airport in order to earn his pilot's license. Thereafter, any aircraft passing over Gross would elicit cries of "There goes Johnny Shular!"

When the Second World War began, John immediately volunteered for service in the Army Air Corps. It was not until 1943, however, that he was able to enter flight school at San Antonio, Texas, where he became a bombardier. The following year, John was assigned to the Fifteenth Air Corps, at the time stationed in Italy and conducting bombing raids on the Third Reich from the south while its companion, The Eighth Air Corps, did the same from England in the West.

When John arrived at Foggia, Italy, in 1944 to serve as a bombardier in a B-17 G, bomber air-crews faced an 89 percent casualty rate. This meant that for every ten aircrew members, nine would probably be killed or wounded go missing in action, or be made prisoners of war before completing their combat tours. Though this situation rapidly improved as the Third Reich was pushed farther and farther back into Germany and its ability to defend itself became weaker, after John flew his first mission in July 1944, he was faced with the fact that he still had to complete twenty-four more before he would be eligible to go home.

Though John never dwelled on it in his letters home or in his diary, the air war he was a part of in the skies over Europe was just as brutal as the ground war being fought below. This excerpt from an account of a mission over Germany by a fellow airman— flying, like John, in a B-17— will perhaps relate a hint of the brutality of the air war over Europe and give a picture of what John faced: Swinging their yellow noses around in a wide U-turn, a twelve-ship squadron of Me-109s came in from twelve to two o'clock in pairs and in fours, and the main event was on. A shining silver object sailed over our right wing. I recognized it as a main exit door. Seconds later, a dark object came hurtling through the formation, barely missing several props. It was a man, clasping his knees to his head, revolving like a diver in a triple somersault. I didn't see his chute open. A B-17 turned gradually out of the formation to the right, maintaining altitude. In a split second, the B-17 completely disappeared in a brilliant explosion, from which the only remains were four small balls of fire, the fuel tanks, which were quickly consumed as they fell earthward. Our airplane was endangered by falling debris. Emergency hatches, exit doors, prematurely opened parachutes, bodies, and assorted fragments of B-17s and Hun fighters breezed past us in the slipstream ... AB-17 ahead of us, with its right Tokyo tanks on fire, dropped back about two hundred feet above our right wing and stayed there while seven of the crew bailed out successfully. Four went out the bomb bay and executed delayed jumps; one bailed from the nose, opened his chute prematurely, and nearly fouled in the tail. Another went out the left waist-gun opening, delaying his chute opening for a safe interval. The tail-gunner dropped out of his hatch, apparently pulling the ripcord before he was clear of the ship. His chute opened instantaneously, barely missing the tail, and jerked him so hard that both of his shoes came off.

He hung limp in his har-ness, whereas others had shown immediate signs of life after their chutes opened, shifting around in the harness.*[1]

John completed his fiftieth mission on December 9, 1944. The diary upon which this publication is based was found in John's effects after his death. With it was an unmailed letter that he had written during the war to his brother, Felix. For reasons he never revealed, John never spoke of them.

Other than the headings of the entries, whose format was changed to aid in clarity, and the correction of transcription errors, the diary and letter are presented here exactly as John penned them. Footnotes have been added to the text in order to explain abbreviations, technical jargon, and instances where the text may be unclear to the reader. These are by no means exhaustive, and any errors within them, be they factual or interpretive, are the sole responsibility of the editor. The footnotes were prepared with the aid of three sources: the first and primary being *Strategic Bombing by the United States in World War II*[2] and, to lesser extents, both *The Strategic Air Offensive Against Germany: 1939-1945*[3] and *The Army Air Corps in World War II*[4]. The illustrations at the head of this preface and the heads of the section breaks within the text are reproductions of the aircraft tail identification symbols of John's wartime unit, the Ninety Seventh Bomb Group of the Fifteenth Air Corps.

---

[1]Ross, Stewart Halsey. Strategic Bombing by the United States in World War II: The Facts and the Myths. (Jefferson, North Carolina: McFarland and Company, 2003): 144-45.

[2]Ibid.

[3]Webster, Charles and Noble Frankland. The Strategic Air Offensive against Germany: 1939-1945, 4 volumes. (London: Her Majesty's Stationery Office, 1961).

[4]Craven, Wesley Frank and James Lea Cate, eds. The Army Air Forces in World War II, 7 volumes. (Chicago: University of Chicago Press, 1948).

MISSIONS 1-26

July 6, 1944 -August 24, 1944

Mission   : 1
Date   : July 6, 1944
Aircraft   : 808
Target   : Verona, Italy

Pilot Slidden.[5] First mission to Verona, Italy. Marshalling yards [6] — accurate bombing. Low element, flying No. 3 position[7]. P-51[8] escort, few fighters; some flak[9] over the right. Toggled[10] those out-twelve 500-lb. GPs[11]. Very light flak— one hole in No. 1 cowling.

---

[7] The waves of bombers the allies sent over Europe in the Second World War were divided into smaller groups or "elements," which were then staggered by altitude and position for defense.

[8] The P-51, a single-seat, single-engine fighter air-craft produced by the North American aircraft company, was arguably the best allied fighter plane of the Second World War. P-51s were the first allied fighter aircraft with the range to escort bombers all the way into the heavily defended interior of the Third Reich. P-51s, along with the other allied fighters that accompanied and protected the bombers on their missions, were affectionately referred to by bomber crews as "little friends" or "little brothers."

[9] German antiaircraft artillery. The term flak came from the acronym applied to the German name of the artillery pieces used to shoot down the high-flying allied bombers, fliegerabwerkanone. Most flak came in the form of an 88- cm time-fused round. Each of these was capable of spewing thousands of pieces of shrapnel into allied bomber formations. Flak rounds need not score a direct hit in order to bring down a bomber. A near miss was often all it took to send shrapnel through the thin aluminum skins of the bombers, disable their engines, cut fuel or hydraulic lines, disable control surfaces, and kill or injure crew members. Losses of bombers to flak during the air war over Europe outnumbered losses to fighters by a ratio of 2.5 to 1.

[10] When mass bombardments took place, the bombardiers would often drop their bombs at the

same time the lead aircraft of their element did. Because a toggle switch was used to drop the bombs, to do so on the command of the lead bombardier became known as toggling. This eliminated the need for each individual bombardier to sight the target through his own bombsight and allowed him to concentrate on fending off German fighter aircraft with .50-caliber machine guns mounted in the nose of the aircraft where the bombardier sat.

Mission   : 2
Date   : July 14, 1944
Aircraft   : 645
Target   : Budapest, Hungary

Pilot Ford. Oil refineries. Our sqn. Flew lowest and last at 24,300. Toggled on element leader but bombs hit west of Danube River. Moderate flak, but we got only seven small holes. One small one in the plexiglass of nose[12]. Black smoke billowing up from a locomotive strafed by P-38s.[13] Six 1,000-lb. demos.14 Flew in vicinity of Belgrade. Our crew flew together. Should have toggled to hit target.

---

[11]A general purpose (GP) bomb. The bomb most commonly dropped in the Second World War by the United States Army Air Corps.

[12] The noses of the B-17s John flew in were made of clear plexiglass in order that the bombardier could see the target through his bombsight.

[13]A single-seat, twin-engine fighter aircraft produced by Lockheed. The P-38 sported a unique twin boom configuration, with the pilot podded in-between the engines along with the aircraft's armament. The design of the P-38 predated the war, and it was largely obsolescent as an air-to-air weapon by the time John was flying over Europe in 1944. P-38s were often, as was the case in this diary entry, relegated to ground attack duties, a mission at which they excelled.

[14]One-thousand-pound demolition bombs. These were used to destroy heavy industrial structures.

Mission   : 3
Date   : July 15, 1944
Aircraft   : 855
Target   : Ploesti, Rumania[15]

Pilot Bombard. Oil refineries. Toggled on leader. Flew No.3 spot in lead sqn. Of group. Only navigator of crew flew with me. Bombs in racks failed to train— salvoed late.[16] Flak moderate, but too many clouds. Couldn't see target.

Mission   : 4 and 5
Date   : July 16, 1944
Aircraft: 080
Target   : Vienna, Austria

---

[15] The area around Ploesti, Romania, contained several large oil refineries that the German military depended on as a major source of refined petroleum for their war machine. Because of this, the refineries were heavily defended by antiaircraft guns.

[16] John apparently meant that the bombs carried in the racks of the bomb bay failed to drop properly. This caused a delay in their leaving the aircraft, and, as a result, they overshot the target. To drop all the aircraft's bombs at one time for any reason was to salvo them.

Pilot Ford. Oil storage on bank of Danube. Flew with our crew, except Dave. Number 2 spot in second element— lead squadron. Plenty rough— too rough for comfort. They got 187 and 258 of our Sqn. Flak rough and accurate. Got Petty and crew plus Hefti instead of Heitz. We were very lucky, in fact, I've had it for five missions— hope it holds on like this. Morrison and I don't get rattled.

Dropped eleven in train, but had to salvo nine on left racks. Bombed marshalling yards as alternate by PFF (pathfinder radar).[17] Cloudy, but didn't bother the antiaircraft of the Krauts. Saw a German fighter go down in flames— later saw a chute going down. Only five small holes in ship.

Mission   : 6
Date   : July 18, 1944
Aircraft   : 513
Target   : Udine, Italy

Bombed Railroad Bridge and a few bombs hit the bridge, but most were over. Really a "milk run"— no flak, no fighters. Were to bomb airdrome in Germany, but because of bad weather, we turn back when over Mont Blanc, and bombed the bridge. We were behind, and a lucky toggle made them hit the bridge.[18]

Mission   : 7 and 8
Date   : July 20, 1944
Aircraft   : 808
Target   : Memmingen, Germany

Pilot Ford. Bombed airdrome with 20-lb. frags.[19] We had troubles; super-chargers had to change inverters or something. Engines regained power, and we went on in.[20] No flak near us and a few fighters, but our 38s and 51s took care of that. Saw what looked like a flaming fighter go down near the Udine Bridge. Pilot Ford. No.3 position in Second element of our squadron. Dog box today.[21] Alt. 23,500— and cold. Flew away from the sun up there. Over Alps.

---

[17]PFF stood for Path Finder Force. One of the lessons soon learned by the United States Army Air Corps operating in Europe was that— European weather being what it was— targets were often obscured by clouds. Because the Norden bombsights carried in the USAAC's bombers were optical sights, they required that a target be visible for them to work properly. When targets were obscured by clouds or smoke from fires caused by earlier bombing, accuracy suffered terribly.

The (partial) solution to this problem was the radar bombsight, which, theoretically, used radar imaging to distinguish prominent features of a target (large industrial complexes, for instance) from surrounding areas. This allowed bombs to be delivered, at least, in the general vicinity of where they were intended to go. One aircraft in a bomb group or element would be equipped with a radar bombsight and would signal the other aircraft when to drop their bombs. The radar technology of the World War Two era was in its primitive, developmental stage, and the radar bombsights used at the time suffered from the accordant bugs and teething problems of any emergent technology. The result of this was that the radar bombsights worked well sometimes, but, most of the time, their accuracy was of little improvement over optical sights.

[18] Each bomber was assigned alternate targets in case something prevented them from carrying out an attack on the primary target. Bombers could attack secondary targets individually or in larger groups depending upon circumstances.

[19] These twenty-pound fragmentation bombs were probably part of larger cluster bomb units. These cluster "bomblets" were especially suited for damaging aircraft runways.

[20] This seemingly minor problem was, in fact, quite serious. If a bomber's engines lost power for any reason, it would be unable to keep up with the rest of the bombers (and their fighter escorts) on the way to or from the target. To be unable to keep up was known as straggling. Straggling bombers were easy prey for German fighters.

[21] Box refers to the "combat box" method of grouping bombers and arranging the groups by altitude in order to maximize the defensive firepower of their machine guns (see appendix C). Dog represented the letter D in the World War Two American military's alpha-phonetic alphabet. Other alpha-phonetic letters used in John's diary are Able for A, Baker, for B, and Charlie for C.

Couldn't crank up the right door, landed with it.[22] A "beaut" for a landing.

Mission   : 9
Date   : July 22, 1944
Aircraft   : 181
Target   : Ploesti, Rumania

Pilot Ford. Bombed the Romano Americano oil refinery. Lots of smoke over the target. Six one thousand-pounders. Pilot Ford, with Palmer (RW) Toma (tail)[23] and McGillivray (radio). Got back later, by straggling. Couldn't feather No.1 as she windmilled.[24] Thought enemy fighters were attacking, but they were P-38s. No. 7 position in the second element.

---

[22] Apparently, the right door to the bomb bay would not close. These were normally electrically operated but, if the electrical system failed or was damaged, a provision was made to close them mechanically with a crank.

[23] The right waist and tail gunner's positions, respectively. These were located behind the wings, and each position was equipped with one .50-caliber machine gun.

[24] To feather a prop (propeller) was to move and fix its blades into a position where they created as little drag as possible should the engine powering it become disabled.

Flak moderate but accurate. Three holes in the nose: one above my head, one in the nose, and one in the horseshoe-shaped glass (didn't go thru both layers of glass).[25] Very slow coming back on three engines, and no. 1 windmilling. Trained out okay. About twenty holes in ship, largest-size of baseball. Beau fighter crash landed on field, probably from previous night bombing.[26]

Mission   : 10 and 11
Date   : July 25, 1944
Aircraft   : 181
Target   : Linz, Austria

Pilot Ford. Two holes in wings. One in right wing about five inches in diameter and left wing had a slit an inch wide and five inches long. No holes in nose. Eureka! Slit one gas tank, but it sealed itself. Ship in the 342nd went down in flames. Seven chutes. 342nd lost two.

---

[25] The very front pane of plex glass in the nose of a B-17 was specially made for the Norden bombsight to view through. The framing of this pane resembled a horseshoe.

[26] A Beau fighter was a twin-engine medium bomber manufactured by the English aircraft company Bristol and used by the Royal Air Force.

Picked up seven holes, only two large ones.
Flak moderate, but accurate. Six 1,000-lb. bombs, GP, Linz, Germany tank factory.

Mission   : 12
Date   : July 26, 1944
Aircraft   : 181
Target   : Budapest, Hungary

Pilot Ford. Three holes picked up. Flak moderate and accurate. Six 1,000 lb. Brought bombs back.

Mission   : 13
Date   : July 28, 1944
Aircraft   : 175
Target   : Ploesti, Rumania

Pilot Ford. Flak accurate and moderate. No planes lost. No.3 position, lead element. Lead group lead sqn. No holes! Twelve 500 lb. Standard Oil Refinery.

Mission   : 14
Date   : July 31, 1944
Aircraft   : 808
Target   : Ploesti, Rumania

Pilot Ford, picked up three holes in tail, one in right wing, one in right side of fuselage, two in left wing, one in No. 3 cowling and one in No. 1 engine cowling. Flak really heavy and accurate. Pitot tube shot out (airspeed indicator) and leak in oxygen on left side. 4-inch hole in right side of fuselage. Xenis Refinery, Ploesti. "Baker" box, 22,800 feet. Smith, navigator, and Michael, left waist. (Twelve 500-pounders!) At least two hundred guns firing at us!

Mission   : 15
Date   : August 2, 1944
Aircraft   : 106
Target   : Portes-les-Valence, France

Twelve 500-pounders. No flak and no fighters. Bombs looked good-on marshalling yards. We four officers flew with other enlisted crew. Bombs trained ok. "Milk run" and we "brought back the milk" (Col. Rogers' phrase).

Mission   : 16 and 17
Date   : August 3, 1944
Aircraft   : 181
Target   : Friedrichshafen, Germany

(Airport-Secondary, Radar). Twelve 500- pounders dropped by PFF and seemed to fall short into Lake Constance. Main target (chemical plant) obscured, so bombed alternate (airport). Weather during the summer has been hazardous and troublesome. No difficulty with ship, except that hands and feet get cold because of lack of heat. 25,800 feet and course was northerly away from sun. Targets to the east are better since heat penetrates the "greenhouse."[27] Whole crew, with exception of Hargis, who's on pass, flew today. L. Waist-Grant. Swiss Alps were beautiful. Lake Constance is on border, half in Germany, the other half in Switzerland. One tiny flak hole picked up. No.2 position in Sqn.

---

[27] At the altitudes that John was flying during his missions over Europe, the cold was debilitating and could even prove fatal for a wounded crew member. B-17s were not pressurized like later bombers and were devoid of insulation to save weight. Frostbite was not an uncommon cause of injury on these high altitude missions, in spite of the heavy leather and wool-lined clothing worn by the bomber crews.

August 4, 1944
Letter home to brother, Felix

Friday
8/4/44
Had $520 sent home from June's and July's pay.
Dear Felix,

Didn't write as good a letter to Rose as I did to Emma since I figured they'd read each other's mail. Have been writing to Dora, Virginia, Barbara, and Lena. Receive the nicest letters from Barbara and Lena, but as Peck says, "I love 'em all." How about his coming marriage?

Got your letter today— took about nine days to get here. There isn't much difference in travel of V-mail, airmail, and regular mail, so write accordingly.

By now, you and Mary must have your diplomas safely tucked away. I haven't given much thought to what I'll do after the war. Will stay in the army if possible. Congratulations on completion of another goal in life.

Will try to write how I feel about combat. Don't have any trouble with enemy fighters since they are at a minimum. Our "little brothers," as we call them (P-51 and P-38 pilots) fly alongside us and keep them away. Have seen three or four 109s shot down by our fighters. However, enemy fighters attack the bombers that have lagged behind. Some get a couple of engines shot up by flak and have to ''land'' on water or lose altitude, but sometimes P-51s or P-38s come along and escort them home.

This flak (antiaircraft shells) scares everyone, especially when you can hear it bursting under you or hear glass shatter from pieces of lead (shrapnel). These shells burst, make a red flame, and break up into millions of pieces. Often, we come home with six or seven holes in the ship and pieces of flak a half-inch thick, half-inch wide and three or four inches long. After seventeen missions (thirteen trips over the target actually, but four of these were double missions), I can consider myself VERY lucky— haven't been hit yet. Honestly, when bombing larger factories, etc. in large cities, the flak looks so thick that when you fly into it you can't see how you'll go through it without being shot down. On a couple of missions, we saw planes shot down on either side of us. Flak usually explodes one of the wing tanks or messes up a couple of the engines. Looks as if you can get out and walk on some of the flak.

Our group has lost some planes and crews, and some fellows have been put into hospitals, but the percentage is remarkably low.

No fighters have attacked our group as yet. Our Ninety-Seventh Group consists of four squadrons. Usually have seven ships to a squadron, twentyeight altogether.

I go to church and pray also. For all of you, all the fellows in the service, and for myself and crew. Navigator really gets scared, and I doubt if he'll go thru fifty missions.

He has nineteen now. Pilot has twenty, co-pilot seventeen, and others have three or four less than us. We officers fly with another officer's crew— gunners— the other day. The trip is a "joy ride" except for the ten minutes on the bomb run.[28] That is hell, and I'm not kidding. Am used to it and figure if it's coming to me, I'll get it!

Since the Germans are being pushed back home, we're bombing the toughest targets possible, and the missions are getting rougher. For a couple of missions, we'll see very little or no flak and then– BOOM— a wall of it to fly to. They must have "master sergeants" or "warrant officers" firing some of those guns- surprisingly accurate. Ha!
Agreed that it will be a nickel" series-Cards and Browns. Glad to learn that Sherman Lollar is doing okay. Why not drop him a line of compliment and encouragement? Write for me too. C/0 Rochester Red-wings, I guess.
Heard Lily Pons and Andre Kostelanetz (her husband) the other evening at a track and field stadium outside of town.

Good living quarters, except that we miss our fountain drinks and good liquor. And women! Have my hair cropped short and am growing a mustache.

Must write Barbara now.

PS— When are you getting married? Heard from Murl and he won't tell me at what place he's located. Would try to find him!

---

[28] For the approximately ten minutes of the bomb run (from the initial point to the point where the bombs were dropped), it was critical that the bomber maintain a constant speed and altitude. Therefore, no evasive maneuvers of any kind could be taken, and the bombers were easy prey for German air defenses.

Mission   : 18
Date   : August 6, 1944
Aircraft   : 855
Target   : Portes-les-Valence, France

Marshalling yards. Twelve 500-pounders. Had trouble with doors. Couldn't lower electrically, so pilot salvoed. No flak, no fighters. Coldest I've been as yet. Feet and hands— no sun up there. No holes in ship and should have been accurate bombing. L. Waist— Michael. Cranked doors up and down twice, but no luck. Must have been switched above toggle.

Mission   : 19 and 20
Date   : August 7, 1944
Aircraft   : 195
Target   : Blechhammer, Germany

(Oil Storage). Eight hours, fifty minutes in length, 660 miles away. Sixteen 250-pounders—Alt. 26,800. Lots of flak, but we were lucky. L. Waist -Dillon. Battle formation (two waves) for first time.[29] Seems beneficial against flak. Actually saw an ME-109[30] shot down by "tail-end" ships of 2nd Bomb Group.

Mission   : 21
Date   : August 9, 1944
Aircraft: 195
Target   : Gyor, Hungary

Aircraft (ME-1 09) assembly plant. Seven hours of flight—475 miles. Twelve 50O-pounders— Alt. 2 3,500. Very little flak-none where we were. Pilot, Maj. Hassler, co-pilot, Ford. Really a perfect day for bombing, and results looked good. Bombed left building of plant. Armament and bombs ok.

Mission   : 22
Date   : August 10, 1944
Aircraft   : 181
Target   : Ploesti, Rumania

Romano Oil Refinery (third time). Battle Formation. No. 914 of 304th hit, gas tank at no. 2 engine caught fire, peeled off, five chutes got out, and later it disintegrated.[31]   Pilot Ford. Co-pilot Fetty. Hargis was back. Petty argument as usual. Henchman stopped them! Smoke-covered target. Flak intense, heavy (guns), and accurate. Battle formation, No. 2 position in Dog Box on left wing. Twenty 250 pounders.

Mission   : 23 and 24
Date   : August 23, 1944
Aircraft   : 331
Target   : Wiener Neudorf, Austria

Bomber Daimler-Benz engine aircraft plant. Kind a cloudy, but little flak where we were. Dropped eight (500-lb.) incendiaries— graycolored.[32]   Two wave bombing. Pilot was Kaufman. Co-pilot, Mellon. Navigator, Chambers. Number six position in cable box. Alt. = 27,500! No difficulty on mission.

Mission   : 25 and 26
Date   : August 24, 1944
Aircraft   : 181
Target   : Pardubice, Czechoslovakia

Bombed airdrome with fragmentation bombs (thirty-eight clusters, six per cluster) Ship 645 has not returned. No flak, but the ship seemed to straggle & fighters hit it. Number 3 position in Baker box. Eight hours, forty minutes— time. Altitude 23,500. Smoke up to 15,000 feet from previous G.P. bombs. Whole crew intact. Boys talked about women until IP,[33] as usual. Thru North-western Yugoslavia, Austria, Germany, and Czecho. Good day to bomb, but no Frag. Tables! Mellon, Straty's co-pilot, went with 645 today.

[29] Apparently, this refers to a further iteration of the "combat box" formation.

[30] A single-engine German fighter aircraft manufactured by the Messerschmitt Company. It and the single-engine FW-190 manufactured by the Folke-Wolfe Company were Germany's primary air-defense fighters during the Second World War. Both were excellent designs and able to contend with the best American and British fighters.

[31] B-17s normally carried a crew of ten. That five parachutes were counted means that five other members of this ship's crew were either unable to exit the plane or their parachutes did not open. Either event meant these men were killed.

[32] Most likely an M-17 incendiary cluster bomb. These were gray-colored and filled with smaller bomblets containing highly flammable mixtures specifically made to start fires. At a preset altitude, the bomblets would be released from the larger bomb casing, allowing them to be distributed over a wide area.

[33] The Initial Point. This was a large, recognizable landmark on the approach to the target where the bomb run began.

MISSIONS 27-50

August 26, 1944 - 9, 1944

Mission   : 27
Date   : August 26, 1944
Aircraft   : 513
Target   : Venzone, Italy

Bombed viaduct with twelve 500-pounders. No flak and no fighters. Wonderful vision and easy target for bombing. Should have knocked it out. No. 6 position in Charley box. Dog usually just below and directly behind Able. Bomb with two waves. Salvoed today because of small target. Six hour, twenty-minute mission. Altitude 16,200.

Mission   : 28 and 29
Date   : August 28, 1944
Aircraft   : 415
Target   : Moosbierbaum, Austria

Bombed cracking plant, storage tank, boiler house, etc. with RDX SOC-pounders (eight).[34] Brought back one bomb. These were high explosive. Squadron lead of Baker box with Gingerich and Ford. All but C-pilot, ball, and left waist flew today. Target was quite clear, but synchronized short on other buildings. Dropped on Able box. Altitude 29,200. Flak intense but below us. Mission at least eight hours long. Nose guns had reverse feed, and double links were backward.[35] Pretty good ship, however. Almost six miles up.

August 31, 1944

Resume
Have lost two crews and a half of Fetty's since we arrived. The 301st lost twelve ships one day at Vienna. The 483rd

lost sixteen ships one day at Memmingen, when we turned and bombed Casarsa Bridge (Udine). The 2nd lost nine ships, August 29 at Blechhammer. One entire box (Dog). Fitzpatrick and Garland (Novak) went down.

Mission   : 30
Date   : September S, 1944
Aircraft   : 427
 Target   : Budapest, Hungary

Bombed North Bridge with six-thousandpounders. Navigator (Scory) screwed up and took us over bridge farther South, made a 360 and bombed the target. We were outside turn, pulling 2,500 rpm and forty-six inches (manifold pres.) but fell behind.[36] Kinda smoky and came obliquely on bridge. Hit over, not so bad. Dropped on my own sight.[37] Dog box (No.3). PilotBieniek. Column of squadrons— a confused Mess. Altitude 28,700 (Dog). Flak moderate and accurate, but not present. Seven hours, twenty minutes. Smith, navigator.

September 13, 1944

Obituary

Mac[38] killed by direct flak hit in lower ball.[39] Right arm practically shot off. Killed almost instantly but managed to turn ball and open door with one hand. #175 and Hinchman flew too. Radio man badly hit and waist hit too. Fragments from exploding ships of 340th hit ours.

September 15, 1944

Buried Mac today near Bari. White cross with name-plate and identification tag.

---

[34]RDX (Cyclonite) was a high-explosive developed during the latter portion of the Second World War; it was more powerful than the TNT explosives used previously.

[35] In addition to the .50-caliber machine guns mounted in the nose of the B-17 for the bombardier to man, the B-17G model had an additional pair of .50-caliber machine guns mounted below the nose in a chin turret. These were also the responsibility of the bombardier and were added to increase the aircraft's defense against head-on attacks from German fighters. The chin guns were supplied ammunition (fed) via a flexible linkage through which the belted rounds passed. It would appear that these guns jammed due to a malfunction of some sort in the linkages of the guns to their ammunition supplies.

[36] Measures of the mechanical stresses experienced by the engines. These were apparently at the upper end of the safe operating range.

[37] John aimed and dropped the bombs through his own sight. Apparently, his plane was so far off the target due to a navigation error, and he was unable to drop them at the signal from the lead bombardier of his element.

[38] Mac refers to Sgt. E. E. McClain of Arcadia, California, who was an original member of John's crew. After the war, John visited Mac's parents in California to offer them his condolences on the death of their son. He is pictured in appendix B with the other original members of John's crew.

[39] The ball turret gunner's position on the belly of the aircraft.

Mission   : 31
Date   : September 17, 1944
Aircraft   : 195
Target   : Budapest, Hungary

Marshalling yards. Mission-Seven hours, 460 miles away. Four (1,000-lb.) bombs, altitude 28, 000. Flak in-accurate and mostly below us. Ball—Loughrey and tail—Toma. Really cold (-40 C.). Two-wave bombing. Good vision and flew No. 2 of able box. Buried "Mac" Friday and missed him today. No holes today.

September 18, 1944
Larson, Strathy's radioman, who flew with Mac and Hinchman, died today.

Mission   : 32
Date   : September 21, 1944

Aircraft   : 324
Target   : Debrecen, Hungary

Marshalling yards. Seemed to hit it too. No. 2 position of Charley box. Target 394 feet high and minimum intervalometer setting.[40] Couldn't salvo twelve bombs, so ball and engineer kicked 'em out.[41] Mission- eight hours, thirty minutes. Thirty-eight 100-lb. Demos. Altitude 21,700. Flak very accurate and moderate. Combat box bombing. Six small holes in ship.

Mission   : 33 and 34
Date   : October 17, 1944
Aircraft   : 491
Target   : Blechhammer, Germany

South oil refinery. Could see nothing, not even the IP. No. 2 of Dog Box. Really a mess— planes all over the sky. Thick cirrus clouds prevented us from seeing able leader. Had to drop bombs by hitting the bomb door switch.[42] Mission nine hours plus. Ten 500-lb. demos. Altitude 28,000. No flak on run but scattered over the undercast. Group diamond. No holes, but really dived out of formation to get away from ships.[43] Pilot—Barker: co-pilot, Freyder. None of our crew. They flew with Morrison. *Barker finished today!* [44]

Mission   : 35 and 36
Date   : October 20, 1944
Aircraft   : 188 (Miki[45])
Target   : Brux, Czechoslovakia

Oil refinery. A short run and couldn't open doors electrically, so had to crank down manually and up again. Flew with Elwell and led Charley squadron. So short a run that couldn't drop bombs on leader. Doors were not opened.[46] Had to land at Falconara airport (Limey controlled) to get fuel.[47] Northeast of Ancona. Landed at 5:00, so stayed overnight and took off the next morning. Got home Oct. 21, at 10:00.

Nine-ship squadrons. Altitude, 27,200. Mission— nine hours, forty minutes. Twelve (500 lb.), Pilot, Elwell, Heilman, Heitz, Goodman. Group diamond— couldn't see target! Flak accurate, but spread out. None of our crew! Colored fellows graciously let us sleep in tents with them. Red flares at Falconara denoting air raid sign. All lights out!

Just like the Fourth of July with all the red flares. Probably an enemy Recon. plane. 620 knots!

---

[40] A timing mechanism on the Norden bombsight.

[41] Twelve of the bombs would not release from their racks and, therefore, could not be dropped. In this instance, the plane's ball turret gunner and flight engineer took the extreme measure of physically entering the bomb bay and literally kicking the bombs free from the racks and out of the aircraft.

[42] Apparently, the toggle switch for dropping the bombs at the bombardier's position in the nose of the aircraft failed and another switch, located in or near the bomb bay, had to be utilized.

[43] The cloud cover over the target was apparently so intense that the pilot of John's plane had to dive out of formation to avoid an air-to-air collision with other aircraft.

[44] The pilot, Barker, completed his quota of fifty missions and would be reassigned to noncombat duty.

[45] Miki refers to the "Mickey set," radar imaging equipment used to distinguish targets when they were obscured by cloud or smoke cover. A bomber carrying this equipment had its ball turret replaced by an antenna for the radar, which was encased in a ball (the "Mickey ball") and lowered from the ball turret opening when in use. The ball turret gunner was replaced by the "Mickey operator" who sat near the radio opera-tor where the controls for the radar were mounted. John's notation "Miki" next to the last three digits of the aircraft serial number in his diary headings apparently means that he was flying that mission in a B-17 equipped with a Mickey set.

[46] The problem lowering the doors of the bomb bay kept John from dropping the bombs on the cue of the lead bombardier.

[47] This target was at the very limits of the B-17s range, so John and his crew landed at a British controlled air base because they would have run out of fuel before making it back to their own base at Foggia.

Mission   : 37 and 38
Date   : October 23, 1944
Aircraft   : 188 (Miki)
Target   : Skoda Armament, Pilsen, Czecho-slovakia

Really hit it with fire bombs! Deputy Group Lead, but took over and bombed by PFF. Complete undercast! Flew Able. Gingerich, Capt. & Freyder, copilot. Heitz was the navigator. Two purple hearts— Freyder, hit in left hand and Heitz, in left leg. Altitude 25,000 and dropped thirty-six100-lb. M-47 incendiaries. Nine ship squadron; another squadron's ship, 709, did not return. Bienik's plane has not returned yet. Gone since Sat., Oct. 14. Got a big flak hole, five inches long and an inch wide, just near my oxygen line, which it bent. A piece lodged in the navigator's seat and another in the fuse box. A hole above my head through the plexiglass. Doors worked okay with the new system.[48]

Gingerich and Freyder finished today. Altitude 25,000! Flak was *intense* and *accurate.*

Mission   : 39 and 40
Date   : November 6, 1944
Aircraft   : 128 (Miki)
Target   : Maribor, Yugoslavia

Deputy Group Lead.[49] Bombed the alternate; were to drop them on Moosbierbaum, but couldn't pick up the target. Bombed visually and each ship had155 hundreds.[50] Gib-son, pilot, [?]elke, navigator. Altitude, 26,000. Gibson finished 49 and 50. Flak was moderate but accurate. Six holes, one in nose. Able box! Moosbierbaum was completely covered by clouds, but Maribor was clear. Just on this side of Austria-Yugo. Boundary.

Mission   : 41 and 42
Date   : November 15, 1944
Aircraft   : 006 (Miki)
Target   : Linz, Austria

Petrol plant. Single ship PFF raid. Altitude 29,000 feet. Pilot, Maj. Hassler, Copilot, Strathy, navigator, Heitz, Miki, Lowry. Coverage from 16, 000 feet up to 29,000 feet. Dropped ten 500 lb., two were delay-action one in six hours, another in thirty-six hours.[51] No nose fuse. Flew into heavy snow twice. Snowed in on Heitz and me, but heated suits kept us warm.[52] Temperature— 52. No flak, no fighters.

Tangent .45. Could see nothing for more than six hours of the eight-hour flight. Prefer this to formation raids.[53]

Mission   : 43 and 44
Date   : November 20, 1944
Aircraft: 537
Target   : Brno, Czechoslovakia

Bombed the third alternate, being briefed for the Blechhammer South Oil Refinery. Flew into clouds, so turned and bombed the marshalling yard. Flew Charley lead, but without a Miki operator. Both me and Baker box were behind and dropped a couple of seconds later than Able. No. 3 was "acting up" [54] and we couldn't catch the lead squadron. Temperature - 33 (quite warm).

Mission   : 45 and 46
Date   : November 22, 1944
Aircraft   : 006
Target   : Munich, Germany

East marshalling yard. No. 2 ship took over, since number one's and our Miki were out. Altitude, 29,200 and dropped twelve 500-lb. SPs. Saw only one burst of flak and group was split up at bombs away because of heavy clouds. . Nine-hour flight. Briefed to fly at 26,000 but went in 3,200 feet higher.

Mission   : 47 and 48
Date   : December 3, 1944
Aircraft   : 491
Target   : Vienna, Austria

Saw one burst of flak. Most of it behind us and late. Strictly PFF. Altitude 29,600-No.l of Dog box. Nothing unusual. Seven 500-lb. RDXs and one propaganda bomb.[55] Three were delay-fuse bombs— two hr., six hr., and twenty-four hr.

Mission   : 49 and 50
Date   : December 9, 1944
Aircraft   : 115
Target   : Regensburg, Germany

No Flak, no fighters. PFF mission. Altitude 28,000. No.2 of Able. Eight 500-lb. RDXs. Delay fuse bombs as usual.

---

[48] The problem experienced on previous missions of the bomb bay doors not operating properly was apparently addressed by its replacement with an improved system.

[49] As John gained experience as a bombardier, he was given more and more responsibility. As Deputy Group Lead, John was the backup bombardier for the entire bomb group.

[50] Fifteen five-hundred-pound bombs.

[51] These bombs were specially fused not to explode until six and thirty-six hours after being dropped. Upon impact, they would lodge deeply into the ground and explode after crews at the target had put fires out or begun repairs, reigniting fires, and continuing to do damage to the target hours and even days after it had been bombed.

[52] As the war progressed and the Army Air Corps realized how serious a manpower threat the extreme cold was to bomber crews, electrically heated suits were developed to help keep crews warm. These plugged directly into the plane's electrical system but were only operational as long as the crew member remained stationary; should he need to move around, he would have to unplug his suit from its electric outlet.

[53] This was a single-ship mission. John preferred it to other missions, carried out by multiple aircraft flying in formation because there was no additional risk of air-to-air collision.

[54] Mechanical difficulty with the number three engine.

[55] These contained thousands of propaganda leaflets. The casing of the bomb was designed to come apart at a predetermined altitude, showering a wide area with these leaflets.

AFTERWORD

After completing his combat tour with the Ninety-Seventh Bomb Group, John was rotated back to the United States, where he married Barbara Trench in 1945. The couple had one child, a son named Alan.

John chose to make a career of the military and stayed in the air corps a total of twenty years, retiring as a major in 19 6 3. During his time in the air corps, John was a bombardier with the Strategic Air Command (SAC) on B-29, B-36, and B-52 bombers. An accomplished baseball player, while stationed in Okinawa, John was a member of the team that won the Pacific championship.

After his retirement from the air corps, John returned to teaching. He taught high school science and business for fifteen years in Southwick, Massachusetts, and was inducted, along with his brother and sisters, into the Kansas Teachers' Hall of Fame in 1984.

John was an avid golfer and enjoyed coaching Little League baseball. He and Barbara split their retirement years between Massachusetts and Florida.

Parkinson's disease claimed John's life in 1996.